BARACK OBAMA

Groundbreaking President

by Jodie Shepherd

Content Consultant
Nanci R. Vargus, Ed.D.
Professor Emeritus, University of Indianapolis

Reading Consultant
Jeanne M. Clidas, Ph.D.
Reading Specialist

Children's Press®
An Imprint of Scholastic Inc.

Library of Congress Cataloging-in-Publication Data
Names: Shepherd, Jodie, author.
Title: Barack Obama : groundbreaking president / by Jodie Shepherd ; poem by
Jodie Shepherd.
Description: New York, NY : Children's Press, an imprint of Scholastic Inc.,
2016. | Series: Rookie biographies | Includes index.
Identifiers: LCCN 2016002661| ISBN 9780531216811 (library binding) |
ISBN 9780531217634 (pbk.)
Subjects: LCSH: Obama, Barack—Juvenile literature. | Presidents—United
States—Biography—Juvenile literature.
Classification: LCC E908 .S53 2016 | DDC 973.932092—dc23
LC record available at http://lccn.loc.gov/2016002661

Produced by Spooky Cheetah Press

© 2017 by Scholastic Inc.

Printed in China 62

SCHOLASTIC, CHILDREN'S PRESS, ROOKIE BIOGRAPHIES™, and associated logos are trademarks and/or registered trademarks of Scholastic Inc.

1 2 3 4 5 6 7 8 9 10 R 25 24 23 22 21 20 19 18 17 16

Photographs ©: cover background: Zack Frank/Shutterstock, Inc.; cover foreground: Pete Souza/ White House Photo; back cover background: Zack Frank/Shutterstock, Inc.; 3 top background: spawns/iStockphoto; 3 bottom background: franckreporter/iStockphoto; 4: Thomas Imo/Getty Images; 5: Thomas Imo/Getty Images; 6: Polaris Images; 9: Polaris Images; 10: Laura S.L. Kong/ Getty Images; 11: Seth Poppel Yearbook Library; 13: OfA/Polaris Images; 14: Polaris Images; 15: White House Photo/Alamy Images; 16: FotoFlirt/Alamy Images; 17: Ron Edmonds/AP Images; 19: Everett Collection Inc./Alamy Images; 20: MCT/Getty Images; 21 background: Lisa Quinones/Black Star/Newscom; 22: The White House/Getty Images; 23: The White House/Getty Images; 24: Jewel Samad/Getty Images; 25: White House Photo/Alamy Images; 27: Larry Downing/Reuters; 29: Win McNamee/Getty Images; 30 background: Orhan Cam/Shutterstock, Inc.; 31 top: Everett Collection Inc./Alamy Images; 31 center top: OfA/Polaris Images; 31 center bottom: Polaris Images; 31 bottom: Ron Edmonds/AP Images; 32 background: spawns/iStockphoto.

Maps by Mapping Specialists

TABLE OF CONTENTS

Meet
Barack Obama

Barack Obama was a child with big dreams. He worked hard, studied, and ended up making history. In 2008, Obama became the first African-American president of the United States.

Barack Obama was born on August 4, 1961, in Oahu, Hawaii. His mother was white.

His father was black. Barack's father was from Kenya, Africa. **Interracial** marriages were not common back then. In some states they were even illegal.

Barack and his grandfather play on the beach.

When Barack was two, his father moved back to Africa. Barack stayed in Hawaii with his mother and grandparents.

CANADA

Hawaii

UNITED STATES

PACIFIC OCEAN

MEXICO

Area enlarged

Barack's mother married a man from Indonesia. The family moved there when Barack was six. Soon after, his sister Maya was born.

Education was very important to Barack's mom. She thought her son should go to school in the U.S.

Barack with his mother, stepfather, and sister, Maya.

Obama loves to play basketball.
He played on his high school team.
Teammates called him "Barry O'Bomber."

When Barack was 10, he went to live with his grandparents in Hawaii. His mom and Maya later joined him.

Barack graduated from high school in 1979. Then he went to college in California and, later, in New York City.

FAST FACT!

As a child, Obama went by the name Barry. In college he went back to his full name, Barack. That means "blessed" in Arabic.

Working for Change

After college, Obama moved to Chicago. He got a job as a **community organizer**. He worked to make things better in poor neighborhoods. Then Obama went back to school to become a lawyer. After graduating from Harvard Law School, he returned to Chicago to work.

BUILT ON SELF INTEREST

UTILITIES DEVELOP

Michelle and Barack pose with their mothers on their wedding day.

Obama worked as a civil rights lawyer. He was a law professor at the University of Chicago. He also got married! In 1992, he wed Michelle Robinson, who was also a lawyer. Later, he and Michelle had two daughters, named Malia and Sasha.

Malia, Michelle, Barack, and Sasha Obama

In 1996, Obama was elected to the Illinois State Senate. He helped make laws for the state of Illinois. In 2004, Obama was elected as a U.S. **senator**. He helped make laws for the whole country.

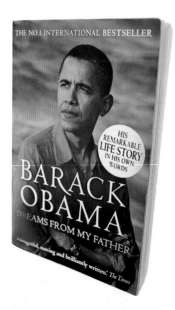

FAST FACT!

Barack Obama's first book, *Dreams from My Father*, was a best-seller.

Obama first gained national attention when he spoke at a convention in 2004.

In 2008, Obama ran for president. Most people did not think he could win. He did not have much money for his **campaign**. And there had never been an African-American president in the U.S. This did not stop Obama.

FAST FACT!

Obama used the Internet to raise money and organize volunteers for the presidential election.

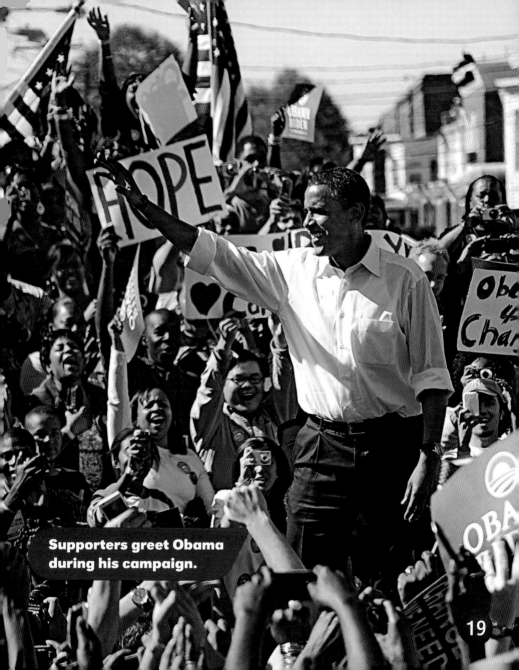

Supporters greet Obama during his campaign.

President Obama

On November 4, 2008, Obama won the election. He was the 44th president of the United States! It was an important moment in history. But there was not much time to celebrate. There was so much to do!

In 2009 almost two million people went to Washington D.C. to see Obama sworn into office. In 2013 (left), nearly one million people were in attendance.

Before Obama became president in 2009, many people had lost their jobs. That meant they had less money to buy things they needed, like food or even a place to live. Obama worked to create more jobs.

When he wasn't working, Obama liked to play with his dog Bo.

Obama also passed a law to make sure all Americans could have health care.

American soldiers had been fighting in Iraq and Afghanistan. Obama had promised to bring them back home. He was able to begin fulfilling that promise.

In 2009, President Obama was awarded the Nobel Peace Prize.

In 2011, American troops started coming home.

Looking to the Future

In November 2012, Obama won a second term as president. He helped pass laws to protect the environment. He also spoke out for laws that would give everyone equal rights to get married.

Obama talked about "clean" energy at a wind farm.

After Obama's presidency ends, he plans to keep working on causes that are important to him. He hopes to do his best to make the world a better place.

Timeline of Barack Obama's Life

1961	1992	1996
Born on August 4	Gets married on October 3	Elected to Illinois Senate

President Obama and his family celebrate his victory in 2012.

Elected
president

Presidency
ends

2004 > **2008** > **2012** > **2017**

Elected to
U.S. Senate

Reelected
president

A Poem About Barack Obama

Obama is president number forty-four—
elected once, and then once more.
We'll remember him—it's not a mystery—
as the first African-American president in history.

You Can Be a Leader

- Learn as much as you can about important issues.

- Listen to the ideas of the people around you.

- Believe in yourself, speak up, and get to work!